Seasons of a Celestial Heart

Sam M.

BookLeaf Publishing

India | USA | UK

Presentation by *BookLeaf Publishing*

Web: www.bookleafpub.com

E-mail: info@bookleafpub.com

ISBN: 9789358314250

First edition 2023

Aries

Exalted in the sunlight
The beams of light pulsing through my veins
I feel the gravitational pull of Mars
It guides me in a way that already takes me there
To the place where I want to be
Bathed in the flame born of white hot dragon's
breath
Feeling alive and divinely guided
The flames soak through my skin
Becoming new appendages of my spirit
Fire pours like fresh paint, ready to drown a
canvas
Then the fire pours like ink, a thousand words
written in blood
Blood spilt by passion and glory
And all along, the pleasure of the pursuit
The pursuit of flame, blood, desire and fire
The pleasure was always mine

Hope Dwells in The Dark

To dim the light of my own soul
As to not shine too brightly
Because to illuminate the room with my
vulnerability
The way the moon spills over in silver splendor
Across a contrasting ocean of celestial darkness
To be that brave in a world so dark
To shine so brightly in spite
To shine with all the light
To be the luminary of my own life
I desperately want to be that alive
That free
That I unapologetically radiate a luminous glow
But I'm afraid
So afraid
That I might just burn myself at the stake
A unique glow sparking a pyre of dreams
All of mine ablaze
To illuminate is to have the world turn in your
direction
All at once
A thousand eyes amongst a thousand stars
Saturn's rings looking upon me with harsh eyes
Mercury has already made up her mind
But I haven't the slightest idea

Of how to make up mine
So I'll hold my light close
Keep it harbored in my heart
Hope dwells in the dark

The Wildness in My Wings

To feel my wings for the first time
To see the sun rise on the horizon line
To watch the world be so alive
And yet to still feel the heaviness in my feet
Unable to meet
The ferocity of my heart
The wildness in my wings
Everything is ready
Except for me
Somewhere along the way
I became too afraid
The stars aligned
And I only looked back
Never watching the nodes of fate
Align with my destiny
Is there still time
To change my own mind?
To spread my wings
And pick up my feet?
There is something so dangerous
About truly believing in yourself
I keep wondering what it would be like
To fall down in a glorious spiral
Leaving everything I ever had
Never touching what could have been

Losing it all
In the world's most spectacular fall
Feeling the push and pull
Of what was and what could be
Finally I spread my wings
Headfirst into the sunshine

Taurus

The magnolia blooms in the rich contrast
Of deep emeralds and pearly whites
An empress among all the blooms
Blooming in hues of Venus
Thick with the aroma of the exalted full moon
A sight of beauty for my tired eyes
Suddenly alive with the moonlight
I drink it like a tall glass of iced tea
The herbal taste taking space on my tongue like
fireworks
The petals falling in orchestrated symphonies
Their crescendos cascading upon my skin in
frequencies I've never known
The world in bloom is a place I've always
yearned to know
Magnolias bloom in my heart
A grove all my own

Gemini

The clouds form in divine formations
Orchestrated by my own thoughts
My thoughts race in nimbus
The thick contoured edges unfolding in all the
shades of the sky
My thoughts like a quill on the horizon line
The duality of the celestial sky and my mortal
mind
Eager to waltz upon the halls of Mercury
Where my thoughts race like children
Wild with the anticipation of summer
The impatience boiling deep within their veins
Angry with the crimson envy of it still being
only today
When there is so much more to see
More to learn in the red sunsets on the morrow
My quill at the ready
Dedicated to not miss a single metaphor in the
glory of the setting sun

A New Home

My hands reach out
With the touch of a ghost
The chance slipping right through my fingers
But the depth of what could of been
I felt that deep within my bones

I clench my fist in protest
But I watch the glass fall
Shattering into the stardust this all started from
I rework how I could have done it differently
Time and time again
But in the end
We only have so much control
There are times when our hearts can change the
world
Then there are times where the universe sings
Her voice strong and beautiful
Impossible to ignore
She changes our perspective
Like the earth being pulled out from right
underneath us
But with that earth that found us, we built
We built something beautiful within the depths
of our hearts
The sorrow that burns deep within our souls

Found residence in a new earth
A new home

Cancer

The moon spills into the sea
Illuminated in the silver silk of moonbeams
Currents finding a home in the comfort of
familiar sandbanks
Comfort in the brackish riverbeds thick with
marsh
These are the quarters of my heart
My heart is but a chalice
Never full, only pouring
A little bit to all who I hold dear
A little bit to all who are within my care
The movement like the tides
Like my tears that well up in my eyes
And falling back in before they can escape the
tide of my welled up heart
But the tide always returns
Like the moon, full and rich with its stolen
sunlight
The silver waves holding me so
Reminding me no matter how low the tide
The sea will always be there to hold me close

Leo

A vision of hope, dreams of desire
The pastels are made of fire
The entire palette a collection of flames
Made of kindling from the lion's mane
Even the ocean blues
Made of the rich salt water hues
Exalted in Neptune
Are born of the flame from the Lions heart
Even the vivid colors of acrylic
Soak the paintbrush freshly dipped
In fire and blood
The texture like pluff mud
The paintbrush drips red in the synchronicity
Of a heart on fire yet drenched in mud
Time and space stand still
My heart beats in lieu of the clock
With the only hope, the only desire
That each stroke of the brush be seen
To honor the voice of my inner child

A Pyre of Wildflowers

The golden hour sets the marsh on fire
Rich hues ablaze in lowcountry wonder
The late afternoon embers dance atop the waters
edge
The embers dance with me too
My heart perfect kindling for this golden hour
flame
It takes hold
Like flora beginning to take root
The flames bursting in synchronicity of late
spring blooms
In the golden hour's glare
It's difficult to see
If my hearts on fire
Or if it's in bloom

I am a pyre of wildflowers

Blooms or flames
Either way
I am consumed by every hue
And forever lost in the view

Wildly Alive

When the rain falls
Gently in the late spring
Summer on its breath
And the world is alive with songbirds
Trees lush and overgrown with late spring leaves
A world in bloom mirroring the musings of my
heart
This is when I feel alive

Late evening sunsets
With that late evening hue all across the marsh,
the sea and the sand
Bleeding reds tangled in deep pinks, illuminated
in the blinding gold as the sun begins to yawn
This is when I feel at home

And how could I forget
The early morning sunrise
The day still so sleepy and slow
But also so alive
As the collective begins to rise and feel each
sunbeam
Align against the corners of their skin
Hanging across the yard in long, stretches
Shadows cast in contrast of the old iron gates

But the stillness of the world amidst the beauty
It takes your breath away

So I will soak it all in
Every hue
Every songbird's song
Every push and pull of my feet in the water
Every sunset and every sunrise
To feel truly and wildly alive.

Virgo

Ruled and exalted in Mercury
The celestial planets hold me in their glory
The honor shines with the intensity of all the
wonder in the world
The honor weighs just as heavy as it shines
The weight makes me stronger
Heavy like boulders of the earth
Wise and old, bearers of honor themselves
They look upon me with sapphire eyes
Their eyes drunk with Mercury
Their shoulders are thick with peridot
The erosion sculpting them like angel's wings
Wide and strong
Ready to carry me home
The mountains form a valley to guide the way
The road to Mercury
Paved in coordination with the divine
I'll meet you there

Neptune's Grace

For every shade of glory
There is a shade of shame
Wonderous miracles
Eclipsed by the weight of the mundane
We are given the choice to embrace the light
Or wander in the dark
But I feel I've always known
Deep within my heart
All the way down
To the bones of my soul
The truth is somewhere in between
Absolutes are stark
Their edges sharp and jagged
I long to feel the smoother edges
Of this world's diverse baggage
Stories of lost loves and other tragedies
Etched into the broken glass
But love will always linger in the moments we
had
Like the sun shining through the rain
Happiness finds a way to smile through
A whirlwind of wonder
A tsunami of sorrow
But to perceive the wonder despite the looming
waves

To dance in the sunshine
And to dance through the rain
Each tear a gentle reminder
From Neptune's divine grace
To have gratitude for the human experience
through every gradient
This is to feel Venus in your blood
And when we are gone
May our memories be passed down
Like songs of the bard
Humming tunes in honor of our hearts
To be human is beautiful in every shade between
glory and shame
I think my favorite is the gradient in between
The slow falling tears mirrored in the setting sun
after a long, long day

That's where you'll find me

Bath Water

Summer's warm embrace
Holds me like bath water
A walk through the midsummer blooms
Blanketed by the humidity of all the stars
Galaxies intertwining with ours
Waltzing with the moon
Almost full herself as she peaks
A moonrise in the garden
She dances in the bath water air
Of the lowcountry summer
Illuminated by sunlight
Singing in the languages of all the stars
The moon falls at sunrise
Just as I close my eyes
Good night
Good morning
It is all the same
When you are intoxicated by the bath water air
Of a southern summer

An acquired taste

Libra

Love is all I have to hold onto
It is all I hold dear
But what I fear
More than anything I've ever known
Is the way the scales fall
When I lose control
I want to hold you in my arms
But I want you to be free
I'm happy to watch you from Saturn's rings
Exalted in the freedom of your own beauty
So that I may feel your love through the
expression of your truth
The range from joy to grief brings peace to my
heart
The way I can simultaneously feel each extreme
Love is in that balance
The balance of the extremes
Find me a noon, find me at midnight
Find me at sunrise, find me at sunset
Venus is there
A treasure of truth
More valuable than all the stars blanketed in an
autumn evening sky

Scorpio

Pluto and Mars dance in the dark
Their faces shadows in the night
My secrets and sorrows sinking deep within the
marrow of my soul
The marrow is strong
Like lava, fluid and scorching
And if you asked, I would cut the palm of my
hand
And I would shake yours like the blood pact of
our ancestors
As they shook hands of their own lava
To find the depth in the intensity
As we find magic in our intimacy
When I feel your heart beating like drums of war
Through the current of your wrist
As I grabbed your hand, thick with lava
Then looked into your eyes
The death and rebirth of your smile with ashes at
your feet
The devil's name on my teeth
And your lips creating space
For a kiss born of the dance
Of Pluto and Mars
Their faces yours and mine
Traveling through time

We've done this before
Again and again in all our past lives
And we'll do it again next time

Cruel Beauty

The world is full of wonder
The depths of which can surprise us
Even after all these years

We think we've gotten it all figured out
Felt the full range of pain to pleasure
Only to be laughed at by the gods
They slap their thighs as our hearts cry out
Falling deeper and deeper into the depths of
heart space unknown
Both beautiful and cruel simultaneously
Harmonious in the inconsistency
Of the greatest pleasure meeting the greatest
heartbreak
Tragedy so beautiful you have to appreciate
The labor of this masterpiece
Every brush stroke so intentional
The way the evening light on the creek
Illuminates the water by the setting sun
The late colors bleeding through the trees
Just off from the west
The vibrations electric, almost like lightning
And I wish I could catch it in a bottle
Save it for later
Savor it forever

Because like the setting Sun bleeding in through
the trees
So does the god's sympathy
Filtered through so well that it doesn't quite
make it through
Fragments wash up in the marsh
Like long lost shark teeth
The reality just as sharp and cruel as their
owner's original bite
Quick, cruel and becoming
Life changing
Wounding
But humblingly powerful in its performance
What can you do?
I'll ride the tides as they fall and return
Try to stay afloat as long as I can
But this boat is collecting water
And it's splashing me at the knees
And all I can think about it how dangerously bad
I want to risk it all and dive under
Abandon ship
Acquire the ability to breath under water
If I could only leave it all behind
Become one with the river
Become the master of the tides
To watch the sun rise from ocean eyes

The world is full of wonder
Extending to depths that can surprise us
Even after all these years

Sagittarius

Jupiter holds my bow
As I take a moment to grow
Yet my determination blooms with my dreams
The bow once a bit too big too hold
Feels now strong and sturdy in my arms
At the ready
I let it go in a deep exhale
My ancestors whispering wisdoms all at once
The world transforming, parallel with my past
lives
Replaying the story of the last time
As the sun rises and sets behind the glass wall
Aligned with my arrow
Ready to take root
With roots likes weeds
Invasive like japanese ivy
But thick with the courage to conquer the entire
south
The air humid with the slow breath of summer
The heat begins to rise
Like hot, burning coals beneath my feet
Nomads don't have houses
No castles or cottages
Just the open road behind me
And the fire at my feet

Capricorn

The goat sings the same song
Up on the hill
Day after day, night after night
For years and years
The goat sings of Mars
The exalted emperor
And he also sings of Saturn
Where I reside
Gazing longingly at Saturn's rings
So far away yet desperately close
So close I can practically feel the ice as it
refracts the light from a sea of stars
The stars asleep in the winter snow
The goat sings still
Determined to finish the song
As I've never heard the outro yet
The crescendo rises but never falls back into
diminuendo
But I've seen the determination in the goats
strong eyes
The power in his voice
And as he climbs the mountainside
In my visions I know he will even climb
Saturn's rings
His voice ringing through the chambers of the
universe

Aquarius

The waterbearer bears it all
Naked in the starlight
Vulnerable in the exposed skin
Strong with the power and courage
To bear the water and bear the weight
Of Uranus's dreams and Saturn's rule
Simultaneously
In synchronicity
A conundrum of honor
The clash of hearts
The marriage of sky
Meeting with the sea
The heavens holding the oceans in their arms
Holding me

The Siren's Wail

How can you trust
The chaos that dwells
In the pools of my own heart?
I thought I knew the tides
The way they rise
The way they recede
I thought I was in control of the push and pull
But the waters are cognisant beyond my own
eyes
Beyond my own mind
With ambitions of their own
Suddenly the tide over takes me
And the waves that once dwelt deep within my
heart space
Break against my bones
Like a storm crashing against the rocky coastline
The tides in unrest
I thought they just swirled within my chest
But I forgot that the seas of my own flow in
channels
A bloodstream of dreams
A dam made up of my own heart
I didn't realize how much I had built up over
time
I thought she was an ocean

The tides pulling in and pulling out
A rhythm
Always on time
I thought I knew her
But she is ravenous
And she is taking me under
I'm eclipsed by the wrath of my own heart
Once I ruled my own heart
A long time ago
But now she rules me

A siren of my own will
My will lost in the sirens wail
All that's left to due
Is to set sail
In my own uncharted waters
The tides inspired by the pools
Of an ever changing heart

Pisces

Is it made of ocean and sea
Or perhaps it's made of dreams
The waves ride with Jupiter
Expanding on the horizon
Expanding within me
As I dive into the sea
I feel as if I've traveled a long way from home
But the ocean sings in the hymns of whales
Exalted in the Venus blues
That reminds me of a home from long ago
To be encapsulated by the waves of Neptune
It reminds me that I am both here in this world
that I've always known
And also returning soon to the place I used to
know
Suddenly the whales singing doesn't sound
foreign
It's familiar
And we sing together
Waves of Neptune and the whales of Jupiter
I've come so far
And when I rest in the comfort of the tide
It feels good to close my eyes
I'll dream of all the adventures again
Waking anew with Mars on my breath